Enough

This book is dedicate to my beautiful family, friends, and people I work with everyday~ reminding myself and others, that we are enough~ what we do is enough~

We are beautiful people just as we are~

.

Compiled and Edited By Mary G. Madrigal, Ph.D.

It doesn't matter where
you have come from or
what you have experienced--

What matters is what
you are going
to do with these
experiences~

-Mary Madrigal

You are **GOOD** enough, **SMART** enough, **STRONG** enough. Believe it and **STOP** letting insecurity run your life.

-Themo Davis

Purple Rose

Surround yourself with
*People who **build you up,***
Encourage you,
*and **Celebrate you**.*

-Mary Madrigal

Rosewallper.com

YOU are GOOD Enough!

Yes you are~

Nothing is *Stronger*
then you~

You are *Courageous*!

-Mary Madrigal

Every great dream

Begins with a *dreamer*

Always remember, you have

within you the strength,

the patience, and the passion to

reach for the stars to change
the world.

-Harriet Truman

Fanpop.com

In Case Nobody Told You Today, You Are Good Enough.

-Spirit Science

Commons.wikimedia.org

I AM ENOUGH.

I am full of sparkle and compassion.

I genuinely want to make the world a better place.

I love hard. I practice kindness.

I'm not afraid of the truth. I am loyal, adventurous, supportive, and surprising.

I am a woman. I am enough. I make mistakes, but I own them

And learn from them. Sometimes I make a lot of mistakes.

-Molly Mahar

You are Amazing

and Wonderful~

-Mary Madrigal

Lord

Enlighten what's dark in me

Strengthen what's weak in me

Mend what's broken in me

Bind what's bruised in me

Heal what's sick in me

And lastly

Revive whatever peace and love has

died in me~

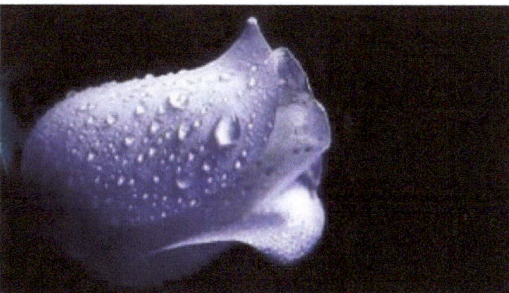

You are *so much more* than Your circumstances~

-Mary Madrigal

Zackavki.com

Don't look back in regret but move on with hope.

The areas of your

struggle or

challenge are not

the summation of

who you are as a

person~

-Mary Madrigal

Amazingpicturesoftheflowers.blog

The most beautiful

Smile

Is the one that struggles

through

Tears.

-Unknown

theGracefulgardener.com

Be Fearless ~Walk Through Your Fear~

-Mary Madrigal

Amazingpicturesoftheflower.blue

NOTE TO SELF.

I AM ENOUGH!

I Love and Honor Myself ~

-Mary Madrigal

Becuo.com

Mzephotos.com

YOU ALONE ARE
ENOUGH~

YOU HAVE NOTHING TO
PROVE TO ANYBODY!

~Maya Angelou

Beautiful-flower-wallpapers.blog

Everyday think of

five things you are

grateful for~

-Mary Madrigal

You will truly

Never be good *enough*

for anyone else *if*

You are not good

enough

For yourself first.

-livelifehappy.com

Pixgood.com

Keep moving forward~

Multicoloredroses.com

"Sometimes the hardest part of the journey

Is believing you're worthy of the trip."

-Glenn Beck

Eddiessolitude.blogspot.com

There is nothing you

Cannot do~

-Patti Leviton, MA

You never know how **STRONG** you are until being **STRONG**

Is the only choice you have.

Acceptance is the answer
to your problems:

I'm **accepting myself**,
my choices,
just the way
they are suppose to be.

-Mary Madrigal

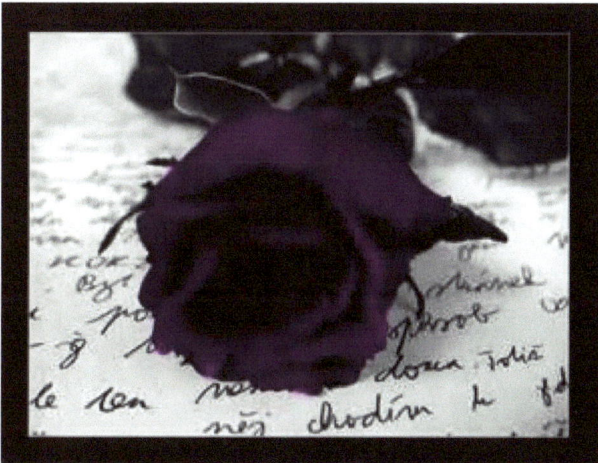

Pinterest.com

Love is the only sane and satisfactory answer to the program of human existence.

-Erich Fromm
Meetville.com

Pinterest.com

Be in the here and now~
Be Mindful~
Be Present~

-Mary Madrigal

Wallpoh.com

Acceptance of what has

happened is the first step to

overcoming the consequences of

any misfortune.

-William James
IZquotes.com

Amazingpicturesoftherose.blog

You are Beautiful and Always have been.

-Mary Madrigal

We do not **Change** as we grow

Older;

We just become **More**

Clearly Ourselves.
-Unknown

The people in my

life *build me up*

and

Encourage *ME!*

We do not believe in ourselves until someone reveals that deep inside us **something is valuable**.

Worth listening to.
Worthy of our trust.
Sacred to our touch.

Once we **believe in ourselves** we can risk curiosity, wonder, spontaneous delight or any experience that reveals the human spirit.

We can all list our *flaws* instead

focus on what is *right with you~*

-Mary Madrigal

Zastavki.com

Acceptance of others, their looks, their behaviors, their beliefs, brings you an *inner peace and tranquility-*

instead of anger and resentment.

-Verybestquotes.com

Take a Chance
Take a Leap
Believe in Love
Your Wings Will
Appear

-Quantum Fractual Energy Mandala

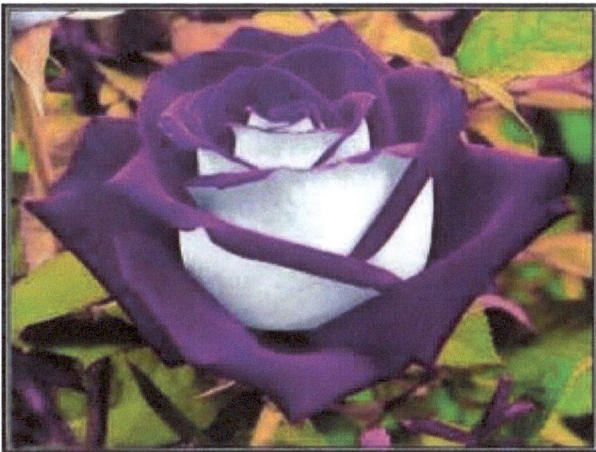

Hdw.com

Acceptance

Have the life you want by being present to the life you have.

-Mark Nepo

Be in awe of yourself.

Embrace all you have come through.

You are
Amazing~

-Mary Madrigal

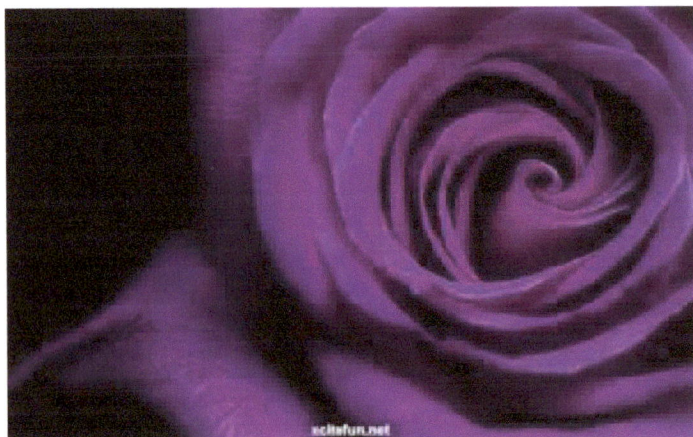

You are *beautiful* ~

Accept Yourself~

-Mary Madrigal

Bestganewallpaers.com

You're a person
oF
integrity *and*
character~

STOP FOCUSING ON WHAT HAPPENED

AND

START FOCUSING ON WHAT'S GOING TO MOVE

YOU FORWARD~

-Unknown

Hdwallpapersinn.com

There is nothing *stronger*

Then you are~

-Mary Madrigal

Ladyluna22.devaintart.com

Do not believe the noises of the world but the silence of your soul.

-GSpirit
-Liora

If you can't fly, then run.

If you can't run, then walk.

If you can't walk, then crawl.

But whatever you do,

You have to keep moving forward!

-Dr. Martin Luther King, Jr.

*You are wonderful
just the way you
are
and always
have been~*

-Mary Madrigal

When you find yourself
cocooned in isolation

And cannot find your way out
of the darkness,

Remember that this is similar
to the place

Where caterpillars go to grow
their wings.

-Unknown

Look around and see the
beauty in your life.

-Mary Madrigal

50best.com

Sometimes you need to walk away.

Not to make someone else realize how worthy you are.

But for

YOU to understand and acknowledge your own self worth.

You might get knocked
down but *you are* going
to get back up~

-Mary Madrigal

From this point on, when I look back on the past, *I will smile* and say to myself, "I never thought I could do it...

But I did...

I *overcame* all the people who tried to bring me down..."

-Unknown

Tapetus.pl

The work I do is

rewarding and

fulfilling~

-Mary Madrigal

Digitalphotography.wordpress.com

Our eyes are in front
Because it's more
important

To look ahead than to look
back.

Don't dwell on things in
the past.

Learn from them and keep
moving forward...

My family and friends
Love me~~

-Mary Madrigal

"*Ask for what you want and*
be prepared *to get it!*"

-Maya Angelou

Keep on *Smiling* at Life~

-Mary Madrigal

Moonangel23.blog.com

When Life Knocks You Down,

Roll Over

And

Look at the Stars.

I am loving myself
everyday~
-Mary Madrigal

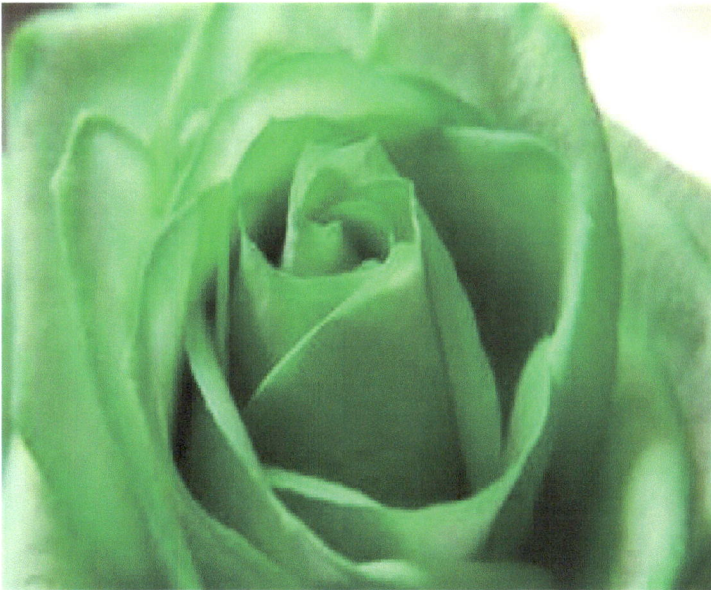

Topwalls.com

Next time you're stressed:

Take a step back, inhale and laugh.

Remember who you are and why You're here.

You're never given anything in this world that you can't handle.

Be strong, be flexible, love yourself, and love others.

Always remember, just keep moving forward.

-Pinterest.com

"The Happiness of Your Life Depends Upon the Quality of Your Thoughts."

-Marcus Aurelius

Artlinethecreation.blogspot.com

Sometimes, you just need
A break. In a beautiful
place. Alone. To figure
Everything Out.

-Unknown

I am the treasure

I am seeking-

-Louise Hay

You are never too old

And it is never too late
to keep

Moving forward in

your

Beautiful life.

I have *everything* I seek~

-Mary Madrigal

Wasafatcleopatra.com

"Be thankful for what you have; you'll end up having more.

If you concentrate on what you do not have,

You will never, ever have enough."

-Oprah Winfrey

Commons.wikimedi.org

Embrace *yourself~*

Jewelsdujour.com

Remind *yourself that*

it's okay not to be

Perfect~

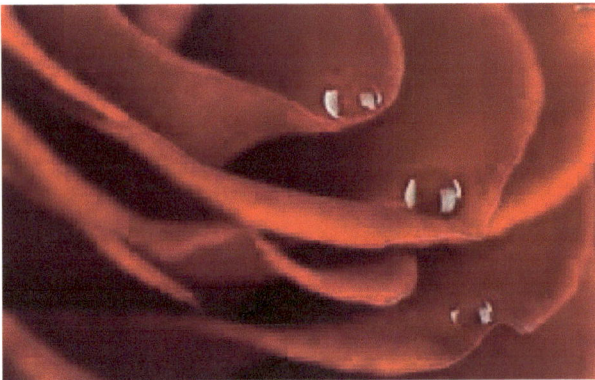

Rosewallpaper.com

You're Perfect Just The Way You Are~~

-Mary Madrigal

I have **everything** *I need~*
Everything I want~

-Mary Madrigal

Courage is being scared to Death,
but
saddling up anyway.

-John Wayne

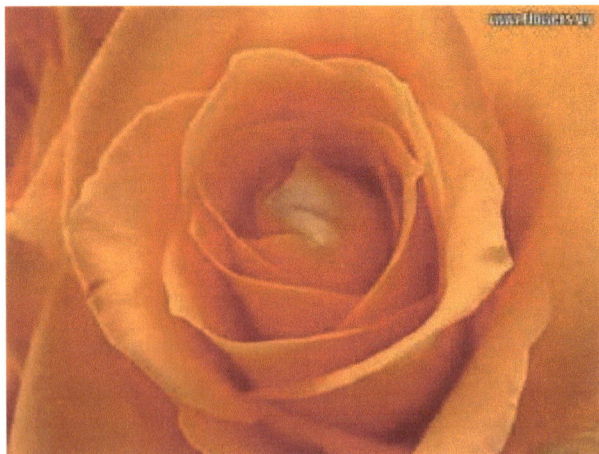

Zuoda.net

Every day you are
striving to be the best
you~~

-Mary Madrigal

Fanpop.com

Self Care is...

- ❖ Speak up
- ❖ Keep Calm
- ❖ Let People Support You
- ❖ Unwind
- ❖ Rest Your Mind
- ❖ Focus the Positive
- ❖ Have Fun
- ❖ Meditate
- ❖ Relax
- ❖ Enjoy the Outdoors
- ❖ Smile
- ❖ Breathe

Honor your process~~

-Mary Madrigal

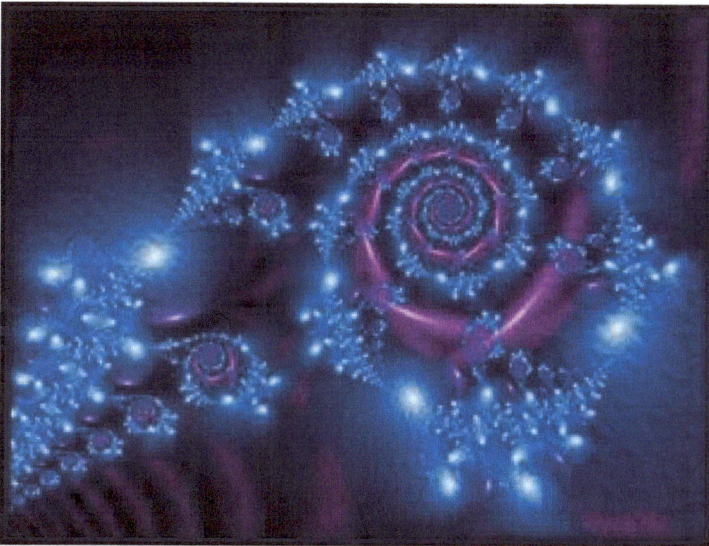

Beautyfullflowers.blogspot.com

"Slow Down

Calm Down.

Don't Worry.

Don't Hurry.

TRUST THE
PROCESS."

-Alexandra Stroddard

Yourswallpaper.com

Everything is fixable~

-Mary Madrigal

Everyone comes with wounds and scars.

Find someone who loves you

Enough to help you embrace your battlescars.

You are loved~~

Ars.com

Spread love
everywhere
You go.
Let no one ever

Come to you without
leaving happier.

Never Give Up!
Never Give In!
Never Surrender!
Never Quit!

-Mary Madrigal

Cakecentral.com

Trust YOURSELF

Because you are an amazing person!

-Mary Madrigal

ebay.com